More praise for Jim Deuchars:

"Surrealism with the heart of a blessed, laughing madman. Deuchars plays with his words, creates language, and never tortures his fabric. A classic car of a volume and we never know if the brakes will work from one page to the next. As Jim would say: *Om*."

-Puma Perl, writer/poet, author of *Birthdays Before and After* and more.

More praise for Jim Deuchars:

"*Mockingbirds Contemplating Semicolons* is a delight. Deuchars' poems are both surreal and eminently readable. The inventive and playful language pulls the reader along, and while you're never sure where each poem will take you, it's always a memorable ride; one you'll look forward to repeating once you've reached the end."

-William Taylor Jr., *To Break the Heart of the Sun*

mockingbirds contemplating semicolons

Poems by Jim D. Deuchars

Kung Fu Treachery Press
Rancho Cucamonga, CA

Copyright © Jim D. Deuchars, 2020
First Edition1 3 5 7 9 10 8 6 4 2
ISBN: 978-1-950380-97-8
LCCN: 2020932923

Cover and title page images: Abigail Beaudelle
Author photo: A. Altman
All rights reserved. No part of this publication may be reproduced or transmitted in any form or by any means, electronic or mechanical, including photocopying, recording or by info retrieval system, without prior written permission from the author.

The author would like to thank the editors of these publiscations where some of the poems in this book first appeared.:

"glossary repulse & petting zoo" originally appeared in *Rusty Truck*. "The Featherbed Dialogues" originally appeared in *Starfish Journal*. "syllables awaiting coffee" originally appeared in *Human Repair Kit*. "fire with fear without fighting" originally appeared in *The Michigan Socialist*. "bad got good (revenge of the cubic cubist)" originally appeared in *Starfish Journal*. "shoulders" originally appeared in *Polarity eMag*. "free verse!" originally appeared in *The Socialist*.

TABLE OF CONTENTS

glossary repulse & petting zoo / 1

ooh ahh zoology / 2

shoofly pi and apple pun darwin / 3

ink pen parasol / 5

Any Questions? / 6

The Featherbed Dialogues / 7

wordling outside lines / 8

translating apricots / 9

Springsign 17 / 11

poets unraveling novelists making things up / 13

onrush homeward, unangelic / 15

riddle-winning window-rhyming / 16

Opposite of Bends (splat!) / 18

smudge stick / 20

occupied / 22

Song of the Trolls / 24

syllables awaiting coffee / 26

that pigeon with the pigeon-shit-stained coloration / 27

unengaging word enragement / 28

they understand these things / 30

trash truck whalesong / 34

truth & beauty / 35

W. C. Fields reads Che Guevara in the Badlands / 36

A Drop of Fog / 38

commercialspace (extra!) / 40

fireflies are lightningbugs (a slorp is an ANDREW
    to a blind harnk) / 41

fire with fear without fighting / 42

from gravy to grave = possibly chocolaty / 43

fugue and far between / 45

Gladys is a dance that is a cha-cha / 46

graffiti growing glitter (jim's not helping) / 47

gone / 48

Hands in Concert / 50

heartbone / 52

Icarus, that's a knapsack! / 53

in this empty / 54

jeopardy leopardspots / 56

watercolor rainbush painting / 57

babylon folksong / 59

april does undoings / 61

it isn't quite / 63

last place i looked / 65

loose as that piano / 66

Lose This Skin / 67

Molecules Betweening Moments / 68

purpling the mexican war streets / 69

addressing whirlpool / 70

after helium / 72

raw / 73

a kid'll eat ivy where a werewolf won't / 74

almost any likely / 76

best foot forward / 78

braying crayons / 80

camelspit in spats 'n spades / 82

wisdom pearl soup bones / 83

words like tug / 85

this machine is left behind to sleep alone at night / 86

Dinosaurs are Organizing Things / 88

mockingbirds contemplating semicolons / 89

this poem is less than the sum of its title / 91

parentheses + poem birdcalls + profane punch lines / 92

even breathing's odd / 94

gracie allen sutra / 95

Buses Only Except Buses (ode to the 54C) / 96

surface tension / 97

chinese mountain poem / 98

This is Where a Pretty / 100

landlord's blade / 102

Riparian Solution / 103

kindergarten, death & other germans / 104

erratica / 106

statuary & suggestion / 107

like yer dizzy / 109

how to scent a girlish lovely / 110

insert martyr here / 111

rockabilly madcap / 112

smoke signals / 113

re: treatise detritus / 118

approximate, like gravity (salt to taste) / 119

Big Sur / 120

super elastic double jimtastic / 122

something we'd / 123

patience imperfect / 125

bad got good (revenge of the cubic cubist) / 126

bubble gumming works / 128

autumn falls a summerful / 129

sound bytes man / 131

drifted / 132

thought that almost was for / 134

Onion Peel / 136

Still Life with Mucous / 137

Snow / 138

shoulders / 139

wrap warp / 140

winter whiskers / 141

wet some frozen / 142

bee sting beat song / 143

And a Death to Stick It In / 144

Rachel Carson Bridge / 145

free verse! / 147

Dime Store Mystery / 148

Dedicated to Daniel A. P. Gee, of blessed memory

glossary repulse & petting zoo

most attention spans are actually pigeons.

most poems are wolverines.

wolverines & underpants.

& freshly showered armpit chicken.

depending on the sense percepted, presupposing that
sombrero is a broken toothbrush (once you
realize that bricks & breasts & broth are different,

you shiver.) saying lazy morning zees
each easy-tonguing lipsmack grape juice laughter
soft as toilet paper trees. casually, denial causes us to think
we be more clever than we often seem to yawn out fetishistic
manifesti. so we orange cone ourselves perpetual, immobile
in an unfamiliar bed the morning after cigarettes
& the broken ceiling fan that rattles
& the wolverines.

ooh ahh zoology

peppertits hides stolen zees
behind his shakespeare.

watch it! when he's in his zone
he's one.

he'd sooner take a shoeshine sober
than pass up chance to fling'em atcha
paper football style.

calls'em shuriken or was it
shooting stars in fish barrel
full of off-key monkeys
and he keeps'em sharp
like mind or cheese
or tip-toe tac.

the stolen zees.
not the off-key monkeys.

shoofly pi and apple pun darwin

it's a beat thrall dance against the angry,
silly rabbit.

it's a simple simon mouthwash rinse:
it tingles.

it's a jump rope skipping
swagger switchback
knee deep in the toe paint,
up to here in hoopla,
whooping wish fulfill
(bewonder) meant to
trip us up in breathless;

entangle us in ivy
staggering to whiplash;

triggering a springsome
heartbeat staging greening
metaphoric set of humid
atmospherics
versing into lyric
summer tendrils

hopeful

nonspecifics left behind
for Universal don't devour

breadcrumb clues i'd
dropped for (nearly)
literally

(her).

ink pen parasol

There's a man dressed in words
so he's suited for every occasion.

His hat and his tie
keep the sun off his eyes
and the soup off his shirt.

His coat's just a jacket
but his pants are his trousers.

He's spelled out his stockings:
kick-tickling shoeboxes-
galoshes galore!

He resents his umbrella of words
(as downright unpoetic!)-
so rare comes rain
made from erasers.

Any Questions?

The word exactly
appears exactly
three times
in this poem.

The word lavender appears
approximately once.

Several words
make no appearance
in this poem
whatsoever.

However
whatsoever
is not one of them.

Centrifugal
did appear at first
but was removed
from final draft.

Described
another way
centrifugal once
appeared exactly
once.

The Featherbed Dialogues

This bible holds no ashtrays,
said the velvet squirrel, subtracting violence.
There's something in the cadence of your pouting
makes me wonder if it's worth the price of oysters.

the swingingest swingset yet whistled
would have none of that!
smirked the Primitive and Restless Soul of Man
And if it weren't for otherwise, he sighed,
how'd I ever get a name like Primitive?

True enough. So true. So yes!
So true enough, again. And still.
said the heartbreak underlying
last night's sunrise,
For what's a universe of bedfeathers
without a featherbed to plant'em in?

wordling outside lines

There's a word on my mind
and when I look in the mirror it's backwards
so I've learned to think futuring tense
to make sense of cartoonish balloons
floating thoughtfully afterwards...

eyeing
symbolic
our silhouette I
for dramatic intense
captivating descriptions
pretending to step on the toes
of events that are happening around us-

that thrill us ecstatic as static-

what steadies us
balancing
beaming
before all
we're happening to
be outside rhyme.

translating apricots

like a furtive curd of beanstalk backtalk
dropping names like bon bombshells;

like a miniature sleighful
or sleight-of-hand soft carbon
cab ride to bliss;

it's a slipknot confusion
carved *NO!* on a swastika'd forehead
and crude as mechanics of time
tend to envelope-steam us
from one thought equation
to next (& twice likely).

or am i thinking of spaceflight?
horse-husbandry? slipper fuzz
comforts of flamespun homefires?

like the parallel sting of song
seen through indigent id-shrouded
aftertease imagery:
bitter hot button bullet point vague-
treading butterpools cream-dreamed &
pigeon-cooped; creeped out; co-opted;
kept; swept under carpets of heartfelt;

left hollow as four hundred 'helluva times', glad-had as hand-me-down all-of-it halfway words caught on the doorjamb; such grapestain misspells all our apricots.

Springsign 17

Dinner bowl is full.
Water's fresh
and yer shitstink
litterbox don't
so why
why
why
the unsound cry
confounding?

Earscratch don't do it.
Belly rub don't neither.
The spot upon your throat
where stroking purrs you
can't be satisfied
(and not just catlike
know how
no how)
so what's this hunger sob
that's got you by the tail?

The march is on,
gone into April.
I saw the smell of green
outside sprung

and opaline like
mallard head

so this must mean
the ant trail's
found your food
again.

poets unraveling novelists making things up

him three-step jig
is dance reactive
meant more tonic
than atomic

him seem p.t. barnum
einstein maned
unkeen unknowing
uncle sam hat-wearing
& handstanding until
edges singed in sepia tone
arrangements of pos & neg
activity alight
this-wayings
to the egress
winking singful

him song hums
love for mixing
greens &
unbecoming red
delicious blues

him bastion of knowledge
and bastard sometimes
and sometimes

bass in college-
collage
him largemouth
pouting technichrome YES
traveling hundred percent
miles an hour
toward true.

onrush homeward, unangelic

a frownful of exhausted nouns
seek boulevard, destructured; seep,
bullish, tasting sideswept streetwise,
neatly, downward; swell to still…
…illogic anxious inching from escape
plan into lockjaw misstep barely redpink stuck
unraveling embroiled roiling honking raw groan
yelping greenish helpfuls flystrip stuck enjambed
at intersect of avenue denude as broken daytime's
promise.

riddle-winning window-rhyming

buzz pop puzzle gossip
sparks across the midnight
airsmoke.

bloodshot half-remembers
mourning spark that
startled it into an almost
dreamless state.

clevering
may scrub it into
clearly

but yer moontooth's
chewing confidence
and mouthing outside
lines of shouted pantomime.

yer drifting misting into better
out of best intentions

whether eastward, western, wily
ripe, evaporating, coming into
hidebound windrush-

wondering if you were ever
even on the roadmap til yer
spunwheel tired trying

drifting onto shoulder
smothering your wonder
til yer gauge (gone empty)
wanders into ways of thinking
habits out until perspective
thrills it third hand definitely
tenderly.

and you recall the way
a smirk can get yer
smiler started.

Opposite of Bends (splat!)

There's an empty playground
Sunday morning feel;

cars pass whitenoise frequent-
churchbound, likely;

but the walkers dog it.
Chalk it up to strolling.

Earthworm squirms so,
comes to writhing;
twisting into dampened black
where mudcrack seeps,
meets concrete table anchor.

Norfolk Southern
railbones R O W
splits park in two
to point us truer

westward

neverminding
do-over logicals;
let alone our overdone
logistics.

Suddenly a narrative
done thread its way
past mindblank
momentary (as
sensation).

Coming down
from clouds,
even when
the mountains
help,

leaves one breathshort:

bent's opposite.

Return to neutral corner.

smudge stick

Getting back to ghostlike:

haunt of spirit
in a scent
more than a
typic apparition

there's a different stillness
like an earthquake
hound dog feels

there's a phantom
gist of it
and all

but all
the while

shrieks of it
are all abouting
all about you

the acrid
iridesces
into awkward-

startling

peripheral.

cold white
at yer
shoulders
shivers
shadow bruise blue.

a little sage'll
broom ya.

don't forget to
scrub yer corners
in the clean smoke.

don't forget to do the ears.

occupied

incant

hazard hush and hightail
downbent razorscram that
thinside almost bettered best
of you go on & get to high
ground hipdeep in too late
already treading moments
then the current has you.

decant

instead of grasping
backplugged
parking lands
amidst a great
unpaving

we bullplow scoured streetsmote
boulevarding traffic moats around
stoned rookeries again.

installed a traffic cop
to guide us round delivery
and installation of the crane
that would install another
mirrored flapjack tower
tinted green

this time inspiring drear
of sidewalks lost to fretful
neon dust for sunshine salve
tomorrow sensibilities.

ratta-tattling workmen echo hammer
jackcut shattering of brickwall into doorway
cutout alley safehouse blindspot vacuum
please remove your hat sir swept into
café terrarium panhandler-free zone
diorama of it's new it's right we understand
a waterfall a cabaret exclusive as we hover over
reclaimed river
reclaims us.

Song of the Trolls

There is another kind of highway sirencall
and I'm afraid that it's an eastern folksong.

These tunes aren't sung on modal western
free range roads but only in the east
where hill meets river to create obstruction
we dare brace ourselves against
for tender BOP! and merrily
we stroll & stew & roil along
until we have afforded
and captured

more-
enraptured
in the BOOM DEEP THUD

truck BOOM
truck BOOM
DEEP BOOM truck

whistlewind THUD
of trollsong pentatonic

in the tuned percussive
undersong of bridge beneath-
a lullaby for feral folk encamped

ping! timbale ping! ping!

bongo auto THUD pong

TRACTOR trailer TRACTOR trailer TRACTOR tractor

skip skip BOOM

S U V DARK pang DARK pang

reverberating HOWLING eMERGENcy eMERGENcy

OUTTA my way OUTTA my way OUTTA my way

whistle pong! pong! DEEP

…as drummed up dreamed across by pace of all its overpassing.

syllables awaiting coffee

when your window opens to the whitenoise
and the dented tincan sparkle of your
half awake awaits your breathing hears your
disbelieving teething exercises
honing words that bark across the page or
make a glancing dash below deck like a
steamship collar hot as doublecross- yer
twice as scared or is it fearful? meddling
in such indecisions can describe a
mind away as ergonomic urge to
blather like a bleating trumpet call or
bleeding unexpected quivering in
fattened hemi demi semi quavers
double wide along the beltline
equatorial whispering flashing
fancifuls we'll halve (we haven't as of
yet). recall unanimous delight at
city streetlight bleaklight stalled against the
blue sky morning mood- a yellowed moment

when sunlight catches razor wire just so.

that pigeon with the pigeon-shit-stained coloration

that pigeon with the pigeon-shit-stained coloration
figuration on its head doesn't really wanna hear
about it from such persons as the likes like me
like pointing out how there's a certain lack
of i'd say subtlety about it's all i meant to
say when i said pigeon-shit-stained

unengaging word enragement

not evil exactly
but a wicked perhaps
in the weekend abstract
dreaming in museumspeak
and drifting shiftless somewhere
pompeii-pompous pious tooth'd
& ruthless juiced ensquoze
ensqueezened looks more
righter. quizic- that be.
thought i'd add an extree
zee but that would be
a torchsong tiki's
third eye of the
worst kind
blind. am i
reminding you of me
yet? sveltish
tongular & longing
epiglottle throttling
baroque disrobing
drops of drab to
sand down
unfixed pearlies
floating easyfree unless
they're leashed and
that's the hazard pay
of reason brazen as

balloonish paisley
posies. here
i plucked them out
myself and offer unto
you a posture or a pose
or make that gentle
resuppose but please no
bookish resuppository.

they understand these things

we're
none of us beyond
our underneath
our cheekbones prove
we're just some wear around it

it's why we put that extra skin upon our first place

as the dawn that darkened
circles naked into
eden aztec aztalan
or stonehenge
our eastern island stoic
carves out new abbreviations
in our rationale for medications

in those good fences making neighbors

& we see the death of webern
in the plastic wrap and styrofoam
surrounding one green pepper

in the thick and running eyeliner
of the hard fucked starlet
who's automatic gasping
porns her pony into numb bliss

it's the shadow secret pantomime
& cause of clown persistence

it's the mask we give the executioner
the blindfold aftertaste
of cigarette gethsemane

it's the cloud of dust
before the part
of hi ho savior's cast
among the clattering of churchbells
like the chattering of squirrels

it's the dream we share our cinematic for
where with all the while in the world
perspective witnesses a modicum of
mimicry at the periphery and
the shot that's blocked before us
is a thing we see instead of be
and there is still a screen between us

that it is
considered hell
to see hell happen
televiewed from distant
others we've consumed-
the crown of bottle caps upon our cranium
kongs us breakfast champions

that it is
considered faith
that what has seemed to
happened

that it seems to happen all the time
that it seems to be a time of some importance
this time
that it seems

that it seems
the oldest trees around us
the ones we've accidently left
throughout our city parks-
the wise ones
who had always
seemed to shrug their shoulders at us
simply reshaped their suggestion
one and then the next
& now it seems that every one
is up in arms

they understand these things
they're more like us than we are
they know these tense dramatic metaphors
are fire escapes held on by their own rust
are the teardrop shapes of arrowheads
are rorschach moments amplifying everything
until we've filled the jar with teeth and nickels

in the way a shotgun isn't always past tense
in the authority of letterhead wearing a belt
to hold it in and suspenders to hold it up
in the hardened heart of pharaoh
and the convenient loss of greenspace

it is what keeps us from complaining
it's the judgment call we made
based chiefly on inflection
or a flip of vigilante football coin allegiance

it's in the subtext of every conversation we have had since
    andrew jackson
and in the spark of sunlight captured in a spider web

it's the stable mediocrity we call experience

it's the consequence of strangulation
hanging out our washing in the rain

and all of it is schemed by such a kind of same
as humans being
you can see the strings
of manlike puppet simile

trash truck whalesong

friday morning measures time
in lots and blocks- aluminum
wrung tinpan siren dumb
struck hollering in whalesong
scraping street on cornered
dumpster:

leaves one wedged between
metallic hollow aftertaste &
plastic thud of heartbeat-
incensed, awake above the
carnival of shook alarmclock
auto non erotic rumbling.

truth & beauty

according to
the time stamp
you hit SEND
on that goodbye
the moment i
was posting
newest lovesong.

that's ok. i lied
about the color
of your shirt.

W. C. Fields reads Che Guevara in the Badlands

GO unto bermuda tell'em how
you love their onions.

lo! and GO to oregon
or idaho & tell'em how
you love their tater tots.

it's a supermarket saturday free sample
smiles by the birthday dozen we shall
tea & coffee through our whiskeyed ears,
banana bread our crumpets
pie our sky with apple pans
and worms'll glow for sake
of lullaby we're all on broadway
now it's spotlight showtime be
sensational

so man GO unto the forest
tell the trees you learned
to tell the trees apart

woman GO unto the mirrored lake
& tell'em you ain't buying in
ain't diving in just yet until
you compensate for rippled
trickster-

knew all along
that was moon
and that was cloud

and there-

Coyote laughing.

A Drop of Fog

Fog drops condense

cling to
tender
tendril
dwarf maple
branch ends

hang

consider falling

hold slow

fattened

warping into
side show
mirror
lenses wide
angling
a perfect
background
teardrop
miniature

like rice
grain
sculpture
spyglass
snow globe
upside
down.

commercialspace (extra!)

manufacturing manifest festering featuring
misfit toy spokesmodel sculpturing
hand gesture shadowplay
socked in the sad cineplexus
and groinstunned fantastic
as fullscreen chop blocked
frozen cookiehouse cut jag-edge
tag-ended candid
to lip of the underfed land
clearly emptied
for an always
availability limited(!)

fireflies are lightningbugs (a slorp is an ANDREW
to a blind harnk)

alligator newsclippings bandages Mirandizing alleycat
fleas crocodiling & tearing at schoolfuls of fishscaling
fleshpot blooms flashpots full ripe with petunias, bananafras
spoonfed untuned bright angelics like popsicles downscythed
and sweet as molasses where fireflies melt flushed brushed
rushed fast (like lightning &) fresh (4 of 5 poets survey the
head of a pin)(cushion) teeth(are 4)cleaning FORE! (half the
fun (of the rinsing's the spitting)

fire with fear without fighting

it's a CON TAME NATION
now they put it in the water.
excess wrongsign redirectives
point us poisoned up we thought
was gravitating down the drainage
spirals. Flush your feverish your
thirsty clench your quench we're
put upon: your DO NOT USE can
further no one's best intentions no one
noticed no one not until the next is
telephonic bedspread readout
mucous miniatures engaged
entanglements of hair: the saga
of our golden skincell microwave
enhancements neon billboard
eyelash fonts for tickle-tonguing:

in our breakfast ON A STICK
interrupting not so news BREAKING
in the transit centers MUST
on the sidewalks DON'T
on the highway DELAY
in our parks KEEP OFF

THIS IS NOT AN EXIT
and you must not P.

from gravy to grave = possibly chocolaty

downcast drib middling drab
last seen gross as lost (promised you)
rights-of-way rightaway!s
fixed in sore-eyed sight
frighteningly halfshell
indenture-framed,

floundering fraud-feeble
frowning (not! drowning
(yet)) saintly as somehow
resizing rehash-browned
halfgrown ideas of flight,
mad as pepper or papermoon
pied pipe-dream peeper
peeks patiently awed (almost
pregnant-paused (this be stiff
way to weightly; full)
awaiting brief naked enchanted
parading passed door-sway ajar
dancing faraway hence (dash of)
dash away madly, thence gone
unto goodly
to godly
to graven
to grave;
lastly:
gravy.

for sake of morale,
our morsel
our chew-toy
our tongue-tied
morality (mostly):

pantomime panda do (barely).
might (may), like as not
spot-on spit-tickle,
bubbling kabuki-blown
gum or bazooka:

shoots; leaves.

fugue and far between

when music surprise you
unwound rounding corners
expecting a blush
smoothly dashed back behind you
ensnaring a smiling heart
skip-rope belonging sense
longing for shock relief
cadence release
as if,
steamed,
advantageous
adventurous us (as we call ourselves) be
at an end all and be
in hypnotic hip post
carded caption proclaiming
unconscious!

Gladys is a dance that is a cha-cha

Gladys is a pseudonym for someone
who's name is not Dolores. She is not anonymous.
Nor even infamous. She is a specific without
need to specify so
we will call her Willow.

Any of these options will suffice.
She has a taste for
consonance at cadence.

Gladys is a name I call myself
is something I would say
if I were in a mood for honesty
and if it were true.

I may might also
gladhand much
in making such
a claim I knew
untrue as if I
felt contrary
typing merry
meaningfuls
to you.

graffiti growing glitter (jim's not helping)

brick mosaic cobblestone
stained glass sand mandala
gumbo quilted compote
miscellaneous-

my plaid brew hodgepodge
montage tangle catalogs composite
checkerboard mélange of wordcube
dominoes on schoenberg's cheesetray.

cornucopious.

gone

were we

had we

would he?

would he still be

here where we

or where he went

where he went still?

had we could have
had we could have gone
had we could have gone
where he went
had we could have
we'd have gone
& would be
gone like him.

where were we?

we were here.

he went there.

were we there
where he went

we would not
have kept him
here.

once he got him going
he were gone and
would have gone
without
or with us
there

but now he is
no longer going
there

& as it were

is gone.

Hands in Concert

Brahms in D minor
feels anxious, sad and urgent.
Manny Ax sits patiently on bench
inspecting swirl of wind and strings-
his patient hands clasped limp,
still.

I sit with someone new-
hopeful, side by side and close
inspecting distance to her hands clasped,
unsettled at her knees.

Manny lifts his wrists-
fingers poised a moment over keys.
I reach and touch, and she accepts
our fingers intertwining each
with unfamiliar others.

Searching to the right of Middle C, Ax is delicate
and tenderly ignores the implication of his name.

I'm learning new particulars of finger length,
anticipating sensitivities
and delighting in peculiarity of palm lines;
worrying my ring is digging into unfamiliar skin;

too soon to know too well-
we're only at our second meet while Manny had
three days' rehearsal with this keyboard
so his searching knows the score.

Softly moving downscale left with cautious joy
his hands cross over- right to left and over/under.

Her hands cross over- resting free fingertips
upon my wrist and sharing impulse.
We lean closer, tighter.

As the second theme begins
Manny's concert hands are winning
o'er conflicted tutti's urgent crying try;
our hands in concert sensing better-
shapes we may fit
falling into…

heartbone

us goes we;
grows is out
could be out
sheer will (come
some *best* betimes
(thrilling! beside self,
decidedly), rhymes: how we
wheelwright our wrinkled
earth-curvature bent (mostly)
skyward (reliably), moon-
beamingly; went heavenly,
heavily metaphor'd;
lent us left-turn time capsuled
perspective: objective(?).

fascination of clear-thought romantics
burns slow from a studied steadfastly:

fantastically.

Icarus, that's a knapsack!

Butterfly wax paper
wings breeze by
brush-stroked
spectacular.

After the fluttering's done,
songing sun-shine;
and the eyelash unbroken
daubed 'wizened'
collapses in hushed tones;
leans chiefly to
whispering side
we'll call fanciful;
musters melodic
what mustn't
be music
at least- not so muscular;

we've spent lungfuls longing,
retuning our fork-tongued expressive
declaratives fueling resourceful
supposing we're all of us
wishing for this
now we're waving
at last

at last
drowned in the fish-soak.

in this empty

i was a poem.

penny copper amber
streetlight orange;

possibly a flickering fluorescent
endangering the epileptics
in the audience;

a shot of ultraviolet in the dark
to make my eyebrown unglue
tilted incandescence much
like saturn shows.

i was a poem
with deep rings
beneath my eyes:

these shadows
are a candle trick of
make-up, sweat and
teardrop rainfall.

lightning flash will thrill you
spilling out your wonder

in a spinning gasp of breathless,
sleepless will-
spent longing;

but sudden green
like fireflies alighting
lifts the tender (three
cheers!) soul of you
to back again.

i've mulled it over and i tell myself
there just might be some otherworldly
in this empty acreage:

so shake off cartoonish grimace
and you'll grapple herewith heartfelt.

jeopardy leopardspots

trick gum lollipop
pepperscotch gag reel
handlebar moustache taped
sideways disguise diabolic(?)
vague scent-balloon dreams taste of
cheddar chalk celery and garlic
like mousetrap surprise
uh-oh! tar paper stickmen jump
bellringing bandage bombs-
some days drum tooth decay
crestfallen shrugs
smugly hopefully bent
dizzy hidden &
hidebound to sweetsmile
your jawbone numb-
tubthump yer skull-
yer chrome shine soul-memory gone languid
as lamp-dancing livewire trip-tasteful and thrilling-

but some days seem pudding-proof
shiftless as downturn's snug gravity
tugs downtown trueheart
dramatic heroics and left-behind
cold-sketched forgottens- no
'thanks for the pretty'

watercolor rainbush painting

rain dapper scampering fog
held in teepeed tents draped over treebranch
topscraping dividing the heat from the breeze
sneezing still

too few drops dewn and fruitful in tao teaspoons due to
such sputtery slipperings unslightly enmeshed
from an 'whence' into frowning confessioned
concoction of spite (as in) spritz of mere spirits supposing
    they're
mists i have known who have left my shirt soaked more than
    this

but i spackle my pridespittle braggery purity purr prone to
    ponder
while moisture ponds into ankledeep inklings much (so far)
less damp than words'll win:
amusing amazing as chance in a brash
faded glance of regretful inference as gauze ghastly ghostly
and dampling my shirt in umbrellas of wet kismet mention

glad wistful gale's garish glowering glow
showers sensibly graced-

for the force fed expanse
of the freewind's palmprint

into faded expansion of drop dwell
expanding to gradual thick
on mine eyelash netbearing-

a puddle of browbeaten
broken umbrellahair

babylon folksong

bubblegum ticklepop pornplum toothpaste
crabapple bittercrush deathtaste shampoo

parachute landingwax grindstone bonesoup
ferriswheel weatherspell inkshower flashlight

ongoing riverbent
hotstove brickstain

aqualung shadowbreath meatscape tattoo
pencilthin spiritrage fickletooth seizure

catalog crownmodel whelpmodest therapy
eyecontact headscour featherfear equity

heavenbuilt housebottom
boatglass bootstrap

morning fences
twirl
spider market
squirrel

speakercolumn razorglass loudshot appendectomy
tidalwave riflecan superhero madstorm

apricot
sensible
apricot
sensible
apricot
sensible

april does undoings

pay attention
what an april
does upon
the ends of things

-the fingernails of trees
untold unfold aswirl befall
in tender outstretch
suncast at last

-one's backneck dander
at it's utmost upright implication
passing strangedog unfamiliars
sniffing sneezing

-the mud pungent hoofbeat
thawprint unfroze smell
abandoned stone
gone wrong

-the low sun peaking out from inside
slung encrusted softcloud dull whose
secret hiding placement messagings
on pencil strength are scribbled
hatless heedless hotair
thought-becoming.

pay attention
what an april
may well do
done unto you
begun at once
& green anew.

pay attention
what an april do
done green.

descending green upon us
momentary breathsweat mossy
lingering as summer forehead dew
believing generally & possibly
our saved-up best
delightfuls.

it isn't quite

there's a cool quality of morning
in the fresh noise
around us
it isn't quite
or yet
describable
as echo
though
certainly
clearer
louder
as if the day
so far
so new
had not yet fully
absorbed the implication
let alone the sounds
of sunrise

like the strange strong
ringing
birdsong
heard nearly
clearly new
but now
grown silent still
for tantalus stirred

i'd seek
to know
identify
unnerve
locate
hiding place
disturb
specific tree
unsuccessfully

sometimes a mourning dove is whistling away

sometimes a swirling pigeon will race the train along

that's the way the words come out sometimes.

last place i looked

Pittsburgh is a broken man
who won't be getting up again-

for doing so would mean
admitting he had fallen…

He generally is true of heart
and hopeful but
his spelling ain't so good-

there's a quality about him
makes you wonder
if he DID mean hopful…

So you can see there is
some cowboy in him-

makes you wonder
what he meant to…

in the first place.

loose as that piano

There you are
spinning my dizzybone
can candor dancing
a song for the roughnecks
(hoot hollerin' extras)
      at edges
sweet slightly and bawd…

          3 and

(for it's time) to
be drunk on
an eye-winking tune
and loose shouldered…

Lose This Skin

She says CUNT! to strangers
and her life is a series of Clash tunes-
in her teens she lived by the river.

Eating nothing that screams
claiming flesh is for zombies
she absolutely hates poetry
and prefers lyrics
growled in Viking.

She's spent time as a stripper
tho she'll use the word dancer-
exploiting exploiters
is fun- (not to mention
she got to work naked)
and now she's as likely to
flash surprise tits
colored rainbow shade
paintings of comicbook
lifescenes-
vagrant confections
of a thousand pinpricks.

Molecules Betweening Moments

There are metal people posed among us;
There are stoic stoned persons poised above us;

in pompeian snapshot
of an everyday occurrence or
outstanding undistracted
mid-behavior

waiting staring
uncontested

frozen just before the point
where reflex habit
turns at once
to bold exalted
memory of a people.

purpling the mexican war streets

there was an echo castaway-
my footsteps' scraping stomp
upon resaca place and reverbed
(dry) to monterey and buena vista,
in the corners, where a wet cold still
enshrouding afternoon's late creep
into castover sunset's purpling of gray
became sunday's silhouetted positive-
that which had been refracted shadow-

around the edges that we couldn't see-

after wind and april coldrain
scared the pants off pittsburgh,
everybody's back inside straight
after church or grocery, lonely
uncle, injured friend or grandma.

addressing whirlpool

places i've lived in or lied about or landed near
on foggy nights of all along ago

i've stumbled on a snowbank here
and there i even did so sober

you serve coffee in there now?
how'd you void the catpiss
disincentive to such custom
as a shopkept café set inside
those walls were listless leaning
wall-eyed once

walked that porch i must've whether
it was boutique then some vintage clothier
who sold me cufflinks or a trim sketch
momentary out from backroomed
alley view apartment strange cool nighttime
longing strange cool blue things sometimes
strange cool far from crowdthrob
staring (sads attached to glances i'd not
pose assumptions on these days)

that brick afronts us building up to first
apartment ever shown to let there was
a bathroom there was crooked outlet
there was that's too big for dogshit in the

stairwell no i'll no not thank you no
such streets such signs of here gone
new then overblown to winsome
back to naked now it's not an untrimmed
overgrowing dead for hidden
broken windows but a handsome arbor
vitae greeting doorbell knockers yes
i mean the clean kind normal even this place
tenable for fortunates or fortunatelys
this was thirty dollar joint i fleabit
through a weekly month or two
until the pawn ran out then i
had to stay at dave's

after helium

in a stretched
stress sense-
deflation.

not of
love/loss
spent

but

scent of
absence

and

the death
of one more
possible.

raw

we milk inhuman kindness
splashed expressionistic
onto brickwall macro-
sex-stained ladling
by bucketfuls
and sizing us
excitable as fools,
slipped our mickey
on a brewing freud-
step staircase
steeped and skittish
as a soap bar
stewing circles 'round
our scruples bubbling
passed our hunger
to aggression
from devour
to more
accidental
anythings
rageburnt
cherry red

so kiss my ashen outlook-

i'm on lookout

and i'm tired

a kid'll eat ivy where a werewolf won't

pottery shards and
poesy bones and
chicken hearts
are rhyming
ticklish arithmetic
and arthritic meat
sweats panting
shredded slacks
and trousers
at the sundried moon
a shade away from
wonderless like
werewolves
and scarred at night
like unbraided light
caught in raw copper
ziploc zipper teething
gear grind (brace for it!)
accommodation of belief
beneath the old man rabbit
fill in shadow picture: HERE
in fine time toonish pruned
uncommon combed animatic
for the neon people
leafblown my way
minding timebomb

signs NO VACANCY in
doom beclouded
awful night

and words like
fang

and
hunger

almost any likely

while lingering
some distance
outside fabulous
awhile, unfocused still
grows whimsy from an empty,
conjures more persuading
meatflesh apparition than a sighing
waterfallen cautionary would
or necessarily even could
seem keen to clue you in
about a promisingly
may have.

technical befalls (tho
rationed sweet on
tongue, a murmur's
less than promissory) no
somesuch sump'n there-

may be silhouette in false dawn-
possibly mirage or beanstalk
shadowstorm or trick of treelight
gleeful

-pause- reflect: redact.

imagine is a biggish thing
'n on the far side (darkly) there's
imaginary nearing real.

halfheart equatorial
laughs it up a hairball
cough primordial
theatrical 'n
almost any likely
or unlikely anything
would fit these physics
shaping mouthstain speculation
kissing polar aftertaste imagine
nearly.

best foot forward

A pair of black Oxfords
broke free from oversized feet;
now rest comfortably
sheltered from the rain
huddled under
London Planetree
cuddling
as if ancestral instinct kicked in
at time of need or crisis.

These are not some sneakers
that stink of death strung-out
hanged and sad
in swollen-tongued suspense
from telephone lines
nor are these the holed-up socks
we abandoned at the roadside.

These men's nines
are fully laced.
The soles are
surprisingly unworn
and they're well-heeled,
to boot.

These are not loafers;
these are useful shoes.
They could use a shine
but otherwise are fine.

Just footloose.

braying crayons

he talked
and thought
in color.
really
he thought
he thought
in color.
mostly
he just
talked.

he pondered tense
until he tensed.
he became high tension
wire skipping clown-
his ballnose somewhere
between maraschinoed cherry
and candy applecore.
his whitepaint face was
somewhere between
sheetrock
and a harder place.
he remembered geographic,
and declared dialectic-
and decided it was drywall.
all the while talking lists
and parsing shades.

he described his shoes.
they were…
yellow.
just yellow.
not piss-stain amber
dandelion goldenrod canary.
just yellow.

mostly he just talked.

and after all that talking
he had charted out the lines
and colored in the space
he'd placed halfway
between grey
and gray.

camelspit in spats 'n spades

sponge yer largeward
wordsplurge purge yer
swollen wallow urge yer
urgent whorl yer hoary
pearl yer purdy swallow
tail to tale or tell yer
all ye ponder then
be wonderful!

wisdom pearl soup bones

When the
fall of falling
leaves us broken
open oaken oyster
fried our dry rot under
shell of tanned intentions
souvenired to gravy boat
we fill with comfort words
we've landed in and on
half expecting
something tugging
on the other end of line
that's left us reeling

we can point
to sign of Oz
Condition several
once or twice each day:

for breakfast,
for example
and especially
on Friday afternoons
where pace slows
to necessity

we learn
and then
accept.

Except we ate the pearl already
and are fishing in the pancake batter.

words like tug

pink limp
ribbon
hung from
underneath
kool-aid candy
dappled
picnic table

mud stained gray
stepped on
unenthusiastic

consequence of death
defying gravity

when only yesterday
there was laughter
all about our heaven
bounding leaping
upward forth &
frothing
shouting
most sincerely
starbright at the
pinwheel center

as balloon stem.

this machine is left behind to sleep alone at night

There's a shovel
on a tractor
labeled CAT
but it isn't very feline
with its gasping
half exasperated
jerk motif
almost a
sickly sway

less than surgical

a plodding wobbly
drowning in the
loud unsteady

tugging groundskin loose
uncrowned
revealing ugly.

Stiff lumberly &
sudden as a drag
steam rollering
was hollering
and hollow
literally

littering &
mongering
a mongrel
approximation
of sandbox
regency.

Dinosaurs are Organizing Things

Birth is sensible enough a way to start
it's where we whelpt the nascent recently
we bore upon this barren earth-shaped body

give my eyetooth ear or other grave appendage

nervous viscera appendix breathing

bones in columns

filling out our hairiness
upbraided wavery
in unentufted tresses
plumed awove arranged
in fabric undressed alligators
immaterial and at last worsted
by a page or two of shapes
we're worn down into
then we're naked flesh
exposed again
regaining regal sense of
(roughly)
all we've eaten.

mockingbirds contemplating semicolons

Splattering
song ring
free range
wordfling
riffs of
unstiff
spiff

; contemplating semicolons.

In the south
and
in the west
and
in all the place names
they are known to flit,
the mostest
strangest
birdcalls
oftentimes are mockingbirds
contemplating semicolons;

oftentimes a mockingbird
who's out to learn your song.

But once
as I was contemplating semicolons
I met a mockingbird
who taught me dragonfly.

this poem is less than the sum of its title

a poem ponders the unknowable.

who would win a fight between
a grizzly bear and
a great white shark?

a poem offers middle ground
between assumptions and extremes.

on the beach.

a poem evens odds.
assures the underdog a fair fight.
problem-solves it.
handicaps, perhaps.

rarely answers.

who would win a fight
between a grizzly bear
and a great white shark

on the beach

if the shark had a knife
and the grizzly bear
was blindfolded?

parentheses + poem birdcalls + profane punch lines

when approximating sunrise
and his (clearly) hello!
morning brightened
noticing admiring
wildflower breakfast
spread of riverslope
yellow feathers sagging

(I know these from backhome prairie walks)

ain't that some kinda sun!flower

past surprising
antique thickwhite petals of
(I'll double check this later- but its
funnel's deep) approximately
ivory blush of wedding satin
(not as blue) with bloodshot
brooding center burgundy
splash stained surrounding
pistil upthrust still antenna

i caress an index finger (almost) handshake
as my fingertip imprints with
(finally!) saffron finedust of this
particular pollen's particulates
i am (naturally)

bound to raise to lips
and blow to samewhite
clutch of bloomful neighbors.

i walk away
good! day

and wonder wandering

when in the act
of mocking hummingbird
(or) proxy bee
(i) be

in some secret shamanistic way-

did I just fingerfuck a flower?

even breathing's odd

perhaps it is the air you cannot see completely through or the se
nse implied that atmosphere is now a solid trees seem snapshot
s of themselves there is a full still pressure even at the tips of hig
hest branches where no leaves sway whispering aesthetic redun
dancies held fast against the taste of stilted mist what would oth
erwise break into song of forehead sweat is left suspended at the
point of undrawn halfbeads for there's no dry space left to escap
e to this is not a time for words like stifling the heavy difficulty o
f most action toward some progress needs more effective effing h
idden deep in words like stultifying and the sudden coolbreeze y
ou think you're suddenly surrounded in on bridge is pyrite pleas
ant tall folktale it will take your breath away exhaling sky as hope

gracie allen sutra

one man's window is another man's ceiling.
one man's door is another man's terrorist.
a friend in deed is an accessory.

don't count your elbows before they're greased.
look both ways when crossing your fingers.
trust after every meal.

medicine is the best medicine.
candy isn't quicker.
laughter is better.

Buses Only Except Buses (ode to the 54C)

cutflower kitchen cabinet
granite macaroni
wholesale merchandise
advertising six packs to go
sheet metal ballet theatre
brass manufacturing uniforms
general machinists
scrap beer antiques
rubber products drugs gifts &
novelties vietnamese
cuisine polish food payday
loans best-made shoes
$1 magic exceptional smiles

surface tension

it's in the moment after waking
fresh from dreaming you

your voice is clearest to me.

while my brain stem basics
barely function
i hear the song you whisper,
clearly.

my eyes
still closed,
i half-expect to
find you next to me.

i can feel the surface tension
of another
on my bed.

reaching for you
i awaken
snoring cat

and now i have to pee.

chinese mountain poem

hiding from the others
in the shed
behind the tavern-
an unexpected stretch
in conversation edges
bottom of your
apple green tee
upways

while bend of leg
against decrease
of shorts
curves elastic
waistband so,
so slightly

revealing point where
hipbone gently rises
then descends.

how many tender
chinese poems i imagined
meditating there
along that crescent ridge.
pondering that valley.

contemplating
time and distance.
even magic.
then lingered there
an extra word
or two.

This is Where a Pretty

This is where a pretty
of a poem
would've happened.
Flutter flattery
aflapping

once it's got your
flabbergasted goat

will gust you
scrumptious-

high to

ain't no even
near enough

almost at least

until gutwrench
wrought unscrews

and groinkick
strips you

thin air breathless

into speechless hover
over blankpage.

& you know
you need to
not to.

& you could
use a shower.

landlord's blade

We interrupt this
everlovin' envied overgrowth
of frenzied ivy tendrils
green furious and
fairly faeried

and the wildflower dancing
fashion blooming
fireflown unchaperoned

for a special
broken concrete slab
deboned axe-throttled
whipped and cutthroat
loose upturned limping
losing laughter
in the slaughter.

Riparian Solution

There
should never
be a river cream.

unless it's made
of butterscotch.

or root beer.

And we
should let the geese
shit where they want to
and attend to other things.

like butterscotch.

and several things this poem doesn't need to paint.

and root beer.

kindergarten, death & other germans

who'll still slanguage slingwise
slung in weightless sleighfuls

wishful dreadfuls

threadbare spoonfuls

after getting's gone
to got-goat gruff
& (scuff my scruff!)
i'm stiff
then stuffed?

be it by whisker or
by tethered thoughtbroom,
doom unspooled, then fooled
my hoofprint proof of pudding's
pop-up weasel goings-on
as fiendish as
it is/they were
forgetful.

preying on a prayerful,
almost nearly any merely
weathers to a soft blank
foam (sic) heavenly

as like as any dogbite salutation
sinks its teeth into the cloudtrough
megaphone miraculous of rabid
night.

erratica

the furious eyelash perspective
the approximate porous that circulates urgent
the freckle illogic cartography

fishgut stockings'll hang
every free born
fur shadow umbrella
yer yardarm
yer nosepick masthead
yer other 'umayaswell'
yer cursive carved escher
entanglements

storm fathom crepuscule
muscle tweaks loudbursting seems

self sustained staindrop
tearfold puckers satin
maps like wrinkled
snowstone
sandglobes
frozen
doomed
to
doable

statuary & suggestion

Make me
outta macramé
or macaroni
twinned in
origami
tissue (two-ply)
overcoat
entwined
with
backbone
twist-
pipecleaner
rigid
legs of
soda straws
and feet of
jumbo
paperclip
trombones
toothpick
scotch-taped
arms attached
with dental
floss perhaps
an acorn hat
(or thimble, in
a time of war)
or matchbook

feathered
headdress
posed
dynamic
diorama'd
in an abandoned
field of bubblegum
and cottonball
confetti
gravel.

like yer dizzy

honey fly tonic pitch
& this type catching
sneezes seizures

scampers

ambers cheese whiz DNA

coughs hiccough's
disconcerting concertizing
chin scratch musings
scuffling effects of gravity
on wind resistance.

screwball turbulence
of peanuts popcorns
crackerjack forth and bop
unnerving dervishing
maneuvers like yer dizzy
was a dean AND a gillespie.

how to scent a girlish lovely

wear a wig of gloves'n such'n-
that'll keep'er offya!

instead,
become a wheathusk crown of corns
or in especially saline conditions
(ie. oceanic): abalone.

oilpaint-stained smock or
overshirt'll stain your turtle
worse than tortoise hair shirt
marks your middling-

best to rill out rhythmic ribcage styling
on a xylophone of mangrove skeletals.

don't beat yerself about yer headphones,
jack, bounding outbound woe reflex
resounding pound of up!hill marching.

blues of sunset stall, settle into indigo until
consistency of ultraviolet smooth is soaring;
snoring; boring into you until yer dumbstruck
stuck in please or pleas or peas.

she leaves.

fast forward to rewind.

insert martyr here

we interrupt your programming
for a viral sense of self sustaining
kidney transplant hatcheries
in bathtub mischief popup
harvest misbegottens
streamed against recurrent
hightide climate
of indifferent whitecell's
strum down blood stream
currencies of pitter
SQUEALthump rattling
loose spirit steering
misaligned rogue tonguing
icecube burntfroze fast
to rusty stitching itch
my scratches

rockabilly madcap

it's a daffodil until the whip-poor-wills it
'cause a tin can can't entrance you quite
like candy can and that's because exciting sunshine
dazzles us dessert words renegade as nuns
who never mind such things
as us and thus from all this suching
much and trifling ragged stupifractious
in the sudden nounsign mustard
whispering designs in moonwax
altru and then all the other isms chasing after it

smoke signals

I
when you come back to the outside
from the underneath you thought
that you were hiding in and now
it's settling on you;

your flying carpet itches;
your magic's just a damp wool blanket
wrapped around another you and sagging
steaming starless.

stop your busi
ness of steering
this contraption wrapped amid
a rusting husk of you

& let it go;

there's a fleeting second part to you
worth flexing.

keep a candle flicker
in the fading roomview
shadows:

it's the fire that will ground you
if you've found you have forgotten
way out of the way in.

II
where wind and water interact
it can be hard to tell where level is-
where surface wavers-
where it bends exactly-

where you'd paced it; where you'd
planned on breaking through

is tangled up in eggshell
shards of dazzle white
kaleidoscopic flotsam.

waterlogged compassion
serves no usefulness as compass;

your breathing sours into pause
that tugs you; urges
sinking feeling til
you're quicksand concrete
statuary for atlantis.

but turn your ear just so:
you'll feel the pulse of wind
disguised as heartbeat;

remember mud of sound thud
traveling in liquid things;

the sweet smoke vapor
whispers just above the surface
guiding you toward sunlight.

this is not the ocean.

so relax

& you will float to top again.

III
when the wildfire
takes out trails you know
overcomes the chaparral
you've sheltered in

images from satellites
and maps online updated
all remind you that your
sacrifice is personal

less so
than it is for
deer roadrunner bear or
rattlesnake

even old coyote

tricked by smell of smoke
that hangs there lapping
at his hightail tempting
hesitation with a taste of
butterscotch and
eucalyptus
with a hint of sage

but it is time
he points his snout toward
salt lick fresh air cool
down switchback

it is his only chance

another playful
godlike dance
of misbehaving
we

gone back to amniotic
& the shelter
of the sea.

re: treatise detritus

at risk mythologics
swimming pools

must from time to time
be drained for cleaning

wounded imaginary
broken glass

must not be swallowed

torn dreamtime pride
bent nails

must be pulled
before they're
straightened

cement sonnets
suns embarrassed
lobster traps
cartoonists' ink
& old men
glue

must set awhile
and think on what
they've said.

approximate, like gravity (salt to taste)

an appealing
dreamweb butter fleshes
apple core imagineering;
deconstructs our tastebuds
(bitter as the aftertaste
of expectation);

combines with savory content of indecision,

tendency of Newton's figs

and the lingering desire
that sweetens words
like satiate;

dulls us into something
more approximate than sleep;

sends us into mouth of day.

Big Sur

when i was young enough
to think that i was older than i was
i dared the crash of midnight surf
while sitting on a driftwood tree
pronouncing thoughts
in recorded voice of Kerouac
slur a-singing
singed in Buddhic slingshot
drumbeat riff & tumble
trembling over 'sorted subji'ts-

mostly how dynamic youthful heroes
die for nothing left to say-
for certain and in no human tongue
and five years passed
before i said another thing

IMMORTAL comes to those
who bray i pray you
in the pitchfork
pitchblack light
of starless ocean dark
beneath those Big Sur cliffs:

you prey:

so winedrunk sit and listen!

to your mouthful surf demonic
and its winded rippling
daring hue of hewn unhuman cry-

possibly the secret voice of golden eagles

the ones jack bloodshot blear-eyed
would've seen angelic

whispering nothing much
about the sadness of the east,
only something of a bigger
death than sadness-

a sadness of perspective.

super elastic double jimtastic

cogent inconvenient unconventional
confessional incongruous
crowned concrete contrapuntal

craving bravely conquer keyless
entry system rhyme scheme
ridgeway tanlines; co-opt
chicken coop cooperations;
hide horseradish insecurities
in such sinful insincerity
almostly
until (as if) ass-up donkey end-ups
motivate the vulture cult of
us to
take to
pigflight fancy.

platypul duckapus
platypul duckapus
platypul duckapus

something we'd

I'll reckon ransom
sometimes
even summarize
in a panromantic voicing
scrawling from the wreckage
of an outline negative
on a stage that's leaving
moving targets outta sightbeams
spitelines innocent of dissonance

-no REALLY-

constructing hopechest songseeds
armed with aimless alms

the consequence of consonance

an odd mishandled fine tune winsome
hairend headstand moment

lemme slap some sequins on yer sequence
or some sense aside yer dizzy stride
yer sunlamp reign's untied

besides

we're not obstructing vowels

nibbling ribbing structure
typewrought rusty in
reconstitutions

we just sample shave
your carpet shag a little
lo hi pile no how!

patience imperfect

time frame
velvet painting
tends to get the
elvis wrong

rush to squeeze in
legshake motion
slurs reflected light
effect to stretch of
jumpsuit when you'd
meant to cheekbone features
unobscured by mudflap
burnsides

too much patience
once too often &
it's tv killing time

you are a cardplay
dogshow leonardo
panting
jesus on his unicorn.

either way

you're breathing traffic
fumes all day

you are a sad
sad clown

bad got good (revenge of the cubic cubist)

I
Math up your practical, cowboy,
I'm meaner than a Chinese midget at pickle carving time
and twice as likely!
I'll tinsel your tonsils boy I'll
dry out yer pomegranate & smoke yer earwax!
You hearing that high pitched medicine yet? Do you
smell something burning? Then drink up those
elbow shavings and nurse your synthetics!
I'll papercut your uncle!
Twice on Sunday!
I'll trap you in parentheses
and make ya call yer parents
so polish up yer Polish
until yer bathtub fills with
treble clefs & toothpaste gravy!
I'll mortgage your meaningful!
I'll mincemeat yer dazzle
morose!

II
well trip my wig and call it molasses!

i'll safety belt your sassafras and
tickle freeze your dictionary
then defrost it for you
with a side of marigolds

and saffron brandycurls
maybe
maybe resod your besotted possibly
let me paint your plumage like a hotrod plum
spice your icicles and
champion your chalk art
hopscotch

bubble gumming works

turtle soup pies ala mode
i've fallen off the beaten carte
and on to thinking thought-riff
outline pics of spinning nifty!

such mischief itch
you've scratched
out downcast iffy-
now it's positively
sharpie-soaked in
spiffy;

quickly,

fetching.

autumn falls a summerful

The part of summer
that's September
stomps you
wearing different shoes each day.

Midday air that sweats you thick
may still come to thunderstorm by sunfall.

Early deadleaf browns and yellows
accent unswept blond brick
sidewalk in the morning.

Sunlight carves clear white initials
in leftover chilly evening breeze
that tempts you into jacket
you'll regret within the hour.

The part of summer
that's September
is a necktie
knotted short
and hanging mid-belly;
a tightening noose
unuseful even to obscure
your overhanging gut;

a touch of hopeful color
temporary-
vivid only in relation
to the darksuit background
it has rediscovered.

sound bytes man

fish hook clearance sale fearsome conspiracies
maybe healthcare or free elections even
enriched like yellowcake white-bred extracts
blue light trance fantastic breadstick schemes
misinformation served informal as the shiver
shake we're shouldering
the malted we've gone molten o'er
the new BOOM fangled crazy
lullaby labelling our red
pyjamas lecherous leftovers
deluxuries boomerung parashot
from frantic rooftops moaning moonbray
scowling at shoestrings cut from wild tusks
for wont of tupperware tinfoil
ivory overnighted smiles
memorizing gumdrops
mesmerizing pigskin pickleheaded us
we're ragdoll's tangled yarnhair we're all
day suckers sniffing fragrant pantomime
and spraypaint roses

drifted

Certain words
birth consequence
when paired
& his were
frail and daring.

Saturday
eroded into
Sunday
morning;
drifted.

He didn't.

Tried to.

Floated into final still
where some would label
finally for it's more than
half-expected quality.

Funeral Director says
it's $1600 up front cash
to die with name intact.

Otherwise,
returned as
unclaimed
freight.

thought that almost was for

As outsiders go
she's a fresh one
dazed awake unfilthy
landed unhooked in the weeds
around the drop-off
dressed in wrinkled yesterday
as if she'd still expected something.

She's hungry
but the hunger hasn't hit her.

That blanket's still her jacket
and those are still the shoes she started with
last night. She may have even had a phone
and friends to wear until she wore out
and was left like quarters- worth the time
and effort to a certain class of desperate,
but mostly an abandoned sock
awaking in a park she may not
recollect collecting in. She's
almost still surprised-

less feral than faithbroke felt
less wild than bewildered

like the housecat caught on screen door's other side-
once the sprung-load snap assures her shut out loud

awake but floating less than clear- a flapping
trout on surface newsprint dream she's come awake above
and vaguely, even realizing now this light's
a side effect of morning; she's likely not a mermaid;
soon she may remember where she left her name.

Onion Peel

An onion peel congealed
last night across the Allegheny
firm enough to stifle shivering waves
and encourage drunken daring.

Firm,
but thin.

Like my confidence across an unplowed sidewalk.

Like the way you say, *It's alright. I don't mind.*

Still Life with Mucous

Building monumental cough momentums
'til I'm near squeamish weakened
like the steamish mist arising
out of fresh'd unfrozen ice cube trays.

Vaporizer's dry cough grumbling hum
thuds dull throat ache until
I may as well spin tumbling rocks
in counterpoint to stomach churning
undigested heating system's rattled rasping turn
and cotton scratch has slow-leak wheezed it's way
to back of throaty breathing's labored pace:
air passages impossibled with SNOT work loose
in pleasant heat massage of shower
melting it along the seams
unleashing Pollack-spackling onto moustache-
even draping viscously across my beard
more impressively composed than Ron Jeremy's
finest Money Shot.

Snow

Whitewash Pittsburgh
hillsides clean, abandoned
as an arctic whaling outpost.

Chalkhill canyons
stoptstill downtown.

Bury Homewood
Cemetery, drift
it to anonymous.

I am the snow;
I cover the grass.

shoulders

rush hour mad chicago
winter sunset honking
christmas yesterdays crowd
shouting bluesongs to the el
near union station pillars
bleary facing west perhaps
awaiting eastbound gauging
lake effect & killing time
but not upon a Rolek's such as this

miscalculating countless
cabs in brandname colors
buses triple parking active shocking
sudden surreptitious doormen
ad hoc busted in their flat step smiles

claiming gifting free intent for helpful!

and the sake of weary traveler!

and I should mention christmas spirit!

and the wrong way river.

wrap warp

silver shards of songlike
light as snowflakes
(dandeleonine as puffball
tufts) swell straggling
supposing whirlgown-
dressed, then thickening to
sweater(better!)like-
conditions' game
traditions

wheregone mystery
gots grown unto enstillish
mist or fitful mittfuls of
delicious majesty or fruitful
miserere or administrative
glad pronouncements
bouncing newborne
Magicals.

winter whiskers

cat fat
fur belly
lump slug
outstretched
loose snooze
purr slunk
upways

whence calm
slips to quizzic
quixotic

from cold froze
to quickly…

…horsefly surprise!

wet some frozen

in the middle of a dusting,
brusque & bristly; queued
to tune of updraft drifting
over sea-shelled ear, white
wash dull flakes damply into
densepack streetside edges.

in the muddle of a misting:
brace for echoing of traffic calls
where snap of brittle nutshell tire
flattens fattened strategies of road

constriction.
in the mystery of mourning
a melt of medicine
constructs a memory
but it is sprung

& so

seeps low
like mudcrawl

underneath a bothersome of wintertide.

bee sting beat song

the grey of overcasted stung sky isn't cotton

balled nor swabbed

this be white of flophouse mattress insides
open sliced for bedtime rat-strung cravings
stashed or outer husk of what may once have
been straw-fluffed sweat-sleep flattened
by-the-week arrangements
inside chicken coop manhattan open-tops

it sorrows up the allegheny
drowsy eastish frozen almost
into bone-sky marrow no
illusion candy sure as sheepcount
shorn marshmallowy effects

nor shaven ice nor cream

but highway snow leftover flecked
suspicious as the peeled banana moon
that upswept clear-scythed portions of the
unkempt false dawn that outslept us

And a Death to Stick It In

Strolling through the Commons
sculpting verse
I pass a frozen pigeon
upturned open-gut devoured
on the snow beside a trashcan.

I cut this moment out of final draft.

Not all poems need to be
another step toward death.

Rachel Carson Bridge

I could write some thoughts on serendipity-

how Engine 32 was passing
at that perfect moment
how the firefighters
radioed to River Rescue
whose brand new
Husky Nattiq Airboat
hydroplane
was stationed
just 2 bridges down.

I could describe
with visceral abandon
the specific quality of
her blood-matted
long blond hair
or the almost
Taoist balance
as her landing
shatters ice
that shatters bone.

But as she lay
wedged
halfway in the
Allegheny
halfway out

a perfect bullseye
centered in a crimsoned
ring of riverskin

all I could think-

she was on the
Rachel Carson Bridge
and then she wasn't.

free verse!

to bring about a world

that's less possessive

to bring about a world

where almost everything is plural

we'll emancipate contractions

and bring suffrage to shortenin'

(we'll be far less 'condescending', too)!

we only need to loose the chains of our apostrophes.

Dime Store Mystery

I thought she walked in
like Ronnie Spector sang.

By the time
she'd walked out

I understood

that she'd walked in
like Ronnie Spector sang
*I Wish I Never
Saw the Sunshine.*

Jim D. Deuchars is an American poet born in Waukesha, WI. He currently resides in Pittsburgh, PA. Dismissive of the tribalism that divides the various schools and cliques of contemporary poetry, Deuchars embraces a wide variety of style, technique, and wordplay to craft poems that resonate equally in academic and outsider circles. Mixed with a generous portion of humor, this results in work that has been described as, *a special brand of doggerel, nonsense & foofaraw.*

www.ingramcontent.com/pod-product-compliance
Lightning Source LLC
Chambersburg PA
CBHW030330100526
44592CB00010B/636